Cosplay

Cosplay

Catgirls and Other Critters

Gerry Poulos

INTERIOR ILLUSTRATIONS BY
Mark Simmons

Stone Bridge Press • Berkeley, California

Published by
Stone Bridge Press
P.O. Box 8208
Berkeley, CA 94707
TEL 510-524-8732 • sbp@stonebridge.com • www.stonebridge.com

Cover art by Daniel Fielding
Pattern illlustrations by Linda Ronan
Original catgirl/critter illustrations by Mark Simmons • www.ultimatemark.com

p. 7   Cynthia Taylor as Catgirl, photo by Greg Heine
p. 8   Krizelle Uychinco as Honey from *Fighting Vipers*
p. 9   Pegasus Maiden as Random the Cat, photo by James M. Schumacher
p. 72 Robert "Sketch" Scholz as Lynx from *Chrono Cross*
p. 73 Ellen D. as Gatamon
p. 74 RikkuX as Original Catgirl, photo by Steve Prue
p. 76 Cynthia Taylor as Rabi-en-Rose, photo by Phil Casper
p. 77 Heather HF as Chii from *Chobits*

Text © 2006 Gerry Poulos

Printed in the United States of America

10 9 8 7 6 5 4 3 2 1   2011 2010 2009 2008 2007 2006

LIBRARY OF CONGRESS CATALOGING-IN-PUBLICATION DATA
Poulos, Gerry.
  How to cosplay : catgirls and other critters / Gerry Poulos.
     p. cm.—(The anime costuming handbook)
  ISBN 10: 1-933330-02-3
  ISBN 13: 978-1-933330-02-0
  1. Costume—Juvenile literature. 2. Handicraft—Juvenile literature.
3. Animated films—Juvenile literature. I. Title. II. Series.
TT633.P68 2006
646.4'78—dc22
                                    2006016012

Contents

Introduction

WHAT IS COSPLAY?

Simply put, "cosplay" (a combination word of "costume" + "play") is dressing up as a character from Japanese animation (anime), Japanese comics (manga), or one of the many video games created in Japan. (Or from elsewhere, as long as it has a decidedly Japanese flair.) Cosplayers create, display, and compete in costumes that depict a given character's appearance as accurately as possible. Since most characters for cosplay are two-dimensional models from animation or comics (some video games are 3-D), creating a costume "in the round" can be a masterful showcase of a cosplayer's skill, resourcefulness, and creativity.

While people have been dressing up as characters for as long as there have been mass media available to present them—modern favorites such as *Star Trek, Star Wars*, and *The Rocky Horror Picture Show* have all inspired notable crowds of fans in costume—the term "cosplay" is unique to the skill of costuming for anime and manga conventions. Nobuyuki Takahashi, a Japanese journalist, created the term when writing about the phenomenon. "I wrote an article for *My Anime Magazine* called 'Operation Costume Play,'" Takahashi recalls. "The editors thought that by creating a new word, they could really draw more attention to it. So we shortened it to 'cosplay,' making a whole new word."

COSPLAY CONQUERS THE WORLD

In Japan, cosplay reached a level of supreme sophistication decades ago. Only recently, though, has it become a major force in the North American scene.

In the early days of cosplay in North America, you might have seen only a few people in costume at anime-themed conventions or events (normally referred to as "cons"). Early North American cosplay was almost exclusively confined to popular anime characters

such as Sailor Moon, because these were the only characters most people knew—it was not at all uncommon in those days for many costumers to be wearing variations of the same outfit. The increased popularity of anime in the mid-1990s and the rise of the Internet, however, changed the cosplay scene forever. Anime became a common sight on television, the cost of English-language anime and manga titles fell, and all of it added up to the huge number of characters that cosplayers in the West portray today. Video games and even card games imported from Japan have become very popular and award-winning subjects for cosplay in an almost infinite (and still growing!) cast of characters to challenge a cosplayer's imagination and skills.

When attending anime- and manga-themed

conventions today, you can now expect to see cosplayers of all types, ages, and skill levels. Cosplay has become part of the definitive convention experience and, for many, the main reason to carry a camera to such events.

COSPLAY AND CONVENTIONS

You might expect to see a smattering of people dressed as fictional characters at any type of entertainment-based convention—a comic book or a science fiction event, for example—but in the world of anime and manga, or Japanese pop-culture cons, it's not uncommon to see 25 percent or more of the attendees in costume. Serious cosplayers invest great amounts of time, money, and effort into their creations. Ensembles can range from simple sets of everyday clothing altered to duplicate a character exactly, to huge costumes that not only require two or more people to operate, but actually have air conditioning, vision aids, and other systems installed.

Cosplay competitions are part of the fun at conventions. Awards are given for everything from best overall costume to best construction or performance. But even cosplayers who don't compete can look forward to the appreciation of other fans. Attending a convention in costume gets attention—cosplayers are part of the show! Wearing a costume means you should be prepared to stop often to pose for photographs and to answer questions about your costume, and that's not even counting the people who will just stop and stare in amazement. If you're looking for a way to make new friends at a fan gathering, wearing a costume is one of the best. It's a ready-made reason for people to come up and talk to you. Cosplayers receive attention from practically everyone, even other cosplayers. And what's not fun about that?

THE CATGIRL

It's probably impossible to know exactly where the idea of a half-cat, half-girl creature came from, but we do know why the Japanese use this ever-popular character often in anime and manga. The catgirl is a simple and effective tool to illustrate the very concept of cute. Catgirls are cuteness and playfulness personified. They are not cats, but humans with catlike traits—this is true even of characters that are aliens of some type. Cat ears and tails are used as a signal to the reader or viewer that the character is, in some way, just like a cat—energetic, curious, or maybe unable to resist something, just as a cat cannot resist a piece of dangling yarn.

THE CATGIRL AS CHARACTER

The addition of cat ears to a female character suggests that she is like a cat—but in what way? Is she playful, or aloof? Haughty, or affectionate? Placid, or energetic? Catgirls can be any age or size, from grade-schoolers to mature adults. They can be sugary sweet or dangerously sexy, story tools or stars of their own shows, but in any incarnation, they are popular. Works such as *Hyper Police* and *Tokyo Mew Mew* feature catgirls as main characters, and popular video games such as *Darkstalkers* take the catgirl to new levels. Catgirls are practically an institution in the Japanese world of art and animation, and to the joy of many a fan, they are here to stay.

BECOMING A CATGIRL

This book sets out to illustrate, demonstrate, and teach the basic skills needed to create catgirls, from a simple pair of ears to tails, paws, and other aspects of the feline persona. These pages will show you the ins and outs of appearing in costume, and give you tips on how to duplicate existing characters accurately and how to simply enjoy being a catgirl. Throughout this book, you will learn the joys and hazards of cosplaying at conventions. You'll learn to get your poses ready for photos and the stage, how to manage your costume, and the dangers of revolving doors, escalators, glass elevators, and other obstacles. You'll also find tips on how to save money on your costume, from where to shop to retasking old clothes.

The most important goal of this book, however, is to help you find your own level of comfort and enthusiasm in the fantastic world of cosplay. Cosplay can be a very rewarding and confidence-building experience and can gain you the respect and admiration of your fellow fans. Most of all, though, becoming a cosplayer can transform you from a simple attendee and spectator looking in at the world of Japanese pop-culture to actually being part of that world.

one

Catgirl Basics

Catgirls are a popular costuming choice for more reasons than cuteness or variety. A catgirl costume is inexpensive, simple to make from a minimum of easily obtainable materials, and open to creative license. This ease of customization makes a catgirl costume the perfect option for new cosplayers wanting to cut their teeth in cosplay and begin their journey to becoming a cosplay legend! The sheer number of catgirl characters appearing in anime and manga provides plenty of inspiration, and you can be sure that other furry cousins such as bunny girls and fox girls will always be a staple in the cosplay world.

GETTING STARTED

Making your first costume will require a few materials. Most are probably readily available around your house, but practically anything else can be acquired on one quick trip to a fabric or craft store. Here's what you'll need to start.

STARTER MATERIALS

- inexpensive muslin fabric (available at fabric stores) or other scrap test fabric, about 1 yard
- pencil, fine-tip marker, or ballpoint pen
- tracing paper or tissue paper or white gift-wrapping paper
- scissors
- straight pins or hand stapler and staples or hot-glue gun (available at craft or hardware stores)
- ruler or tape measure
- cotton batting or foam pillow stuffing (available at fabric stores)
- sewing needle and thread
- fabric for finished costume pieces—preferably felt, velvet, or fake fur, about 1 yard

Cosplaying on a Budget Cosplay doesn't have to be expensive! You can reuse things that you already have, such as old T-shirts, to practice your sewing skills before spending a dime. Go through your closet and drawers and search for things you never wear anymore, or ask your family to let you go through all those boxes of forgotten stuff in the basement, attic, or garage. Who knows what you might find there that can be reused? Secondhand stores and thrift stores are also a boon to cosplayers looking to cut costs. Thrift stores can yield yards of very expensive and hard-to-get materials and ready-made clothing for mere pennies on the dollar. And think ahead—can you use the same wig on more than one costume? How about the shoes? Can one costume be cut down, or reworked into another?

CREATING EASY PATTERNS

At first, pattern making can sound like a daunting or even frightening prospect, but it's really not. A pattern is simply a blueprint to what you want to make, showing the size and shape, where you will cut, and where you will sew. Making a pattern first will save you time and money in the long run, especially if you plan to use expensive fabric. It's better to work out the details of your design at the pattern stage than find out what doesn't work through trial and error. A good pattern can eliminate costly mistakes.

For your first pair of ears, you'll want to make a test version out of an inexpensive material such as muslin (a plain cotton fabric of the type typically used for sheets) before proceeding on to work with your good fabric. Any fabric store, or even a more general outlet store such as Wal-Mart, has muslin for sale for only a few dollars a yard. It is unlikely that you'll need more than a single yard of material to create a pair of ears, or even several pairs, if you end up making more than one test. And you can use any leftover material to make tests of other parts of your costume, such as the tail and paws.

Alternatively, you can make your test on a piece of sturdy, non-stretch material that you may have lying around your house, such as an old stained shirt or bed sheet. Heavy material such as corduroy or denim is not recommended because it's harder to work with and won't be as easy to adjust while fine-tuning your creation. Likewise, avoid stretchy or ribbed fabrics. Stretch material will have too much "give," and a pattern made from it will likely end up distorted, puckered, or deformed-looking.

You'll want tracing paper on which to make your patterns. Tissue paper or thin

Basic Sewing Any costume that you want to wear more than once, or to keep, you'll want to sew together, either by hand or on a sewing machine. Small items like ears can easily be done by hand, but for larger items, like tails, a sewing machine greatly speeds up the process. If you've never worked with a sewing machine before and plan to get into any kind of serious tailoring or dressmaking work, it's a good idea to take a sewing class so that you can take advantage of the extra features available to you with a machine. If you're not that interested in sewing, and just want to make a simple costume, the only sewing skills you will need are the ability to thread a needle, to do a simple straight stitch, and to tie off the thread when you're done.

white gift-wrapping paper can also work well (drugstores, stationery stores, or office supply stores are all good sources for these), but whatever you use, make sure it's thin enough to be translucent, as you'll need to be able to see through it to copy the lines on the pattern to the fabric underneath. You'll also want a pair of scissors on hand, a tape measure or ruler, and some straight pins (also to be found wherever you buy fabric), or as an alternative to pins that you might find fun and easy—a stapler.

Staples, as a replacement for sewing, can speed up the process of making your muslin test immensely. Using this method, a pair of ears can be constructed in less than five minutes! Staples are also a good choice for beginning cosplayers because they won't prick your fingers as pins will, and being stronger than pins, won't fall out. However, staples are only really useful for initial tests or quick costumes that you don't plan to wear more than once or twice—anything you want to keep for a long time (or plan to eventually wash!) should be sewn with a needle and thread. Staples will tear through thin fabric if put under too much stress, and water will make them rust.

Another method for making muslin tests is a hot-glue gun, which can be found in nearly any craft store, home supply store, or hard-ware store. Hot glue is not suitable for a finished costume, but for making a test it should work fine. (Be sure to follow all the manufacturer's instructions when using hot glue, as it is, very literally, hot, and can burn your fingers if you're not careful.) The drawback of using a glue gun as opposed to staples is that staples can be easily removed and repositioned to make adjustments, whereas once glue has been used to stick pieces together . . . you're stuck. Hot glue is only truly useful when you feel fairly sure of your pattern and don't expect to have to make many adjustments to the shape.

The Two Sides of Fabric Most fabrics have a finished side and an unfinished "rough" side. This is particularly noticeable with heavy fabrics, such as fake furs or velvets. Remember that when sewing, you will always want to make sure to draw all of your pattern lines on the rough side of the material, as this is the side you will be doing all of your sewing work on. Then, once the pieces are sewn together, you will be turning the fabric right-side out, so the finished side faces outward and all of your sew lines or staples are hidden.

STEP BY STEP

BASIC CAT EARS

Catgirls come in many shapes and forms, but all catgirls have one major thing in common—prominent ears. No matter what else you're wearing, a pair of ears turns you instantly into a bona fide catgirl. That fact alone probably explains to a large degree the popularity of catgirl cosplay—You can't get much easier than a simple pair of ears! Here's how to make a very basic set of ears that can be attached to your head with bobby pins.

This is a basic ear pattern. Trace this pattern onto a piece of tracing paper and carefully cut out the tracing along the outside lines.

1 Place the cutout—this is your template—onto the "rough," not "finished," side of a piece of material with at least ½ inch extra space all around the template. Trace around the template onto the piece of material with a pencil or pen.

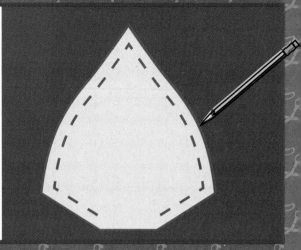

2 Copy the inside line of the template onto the fabric. An easy way to do this is to poke small holes through your paper pattern along the inner line to transfer a dotted line onto the fabric. This will be your sewing line, where you will be stitching the fabric. Repeat steps 1 and 2 until you have 4 pieces outlined.

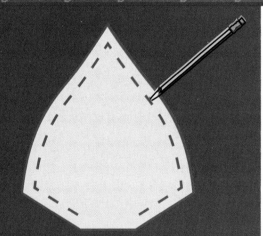

3 Carefully cut out the pieces along the outside lines, making your initial cuts just a little bigger than the rough line you've drawn. Stack all 4 pieces of material together and trim with scissors until all 4 pieces are the same. Separate the material into 2 pairs and arrange the pairs with the finished sides facing each other, "rough" sides with the marks facing out.

Result

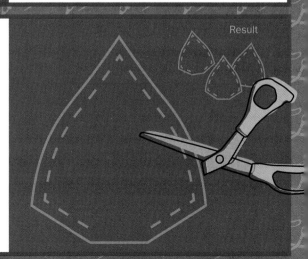

4 Pick up 1 pair of pieces. Make sure the lines are on top (both sides), the "rough" sides facing out. Using a stapler or pins, join the pieces together along the inside line. Leave the bottom edge open. Repeat with the second pair of material pieces. If things don't look quite right, just remove the staples or pins and reposition.

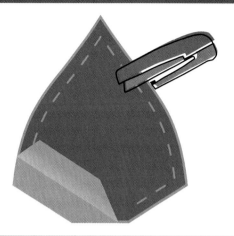

5 Once the material is joined together, turn the ears inside out—or actually, right side out. This will put the "finished" side of the fabric on the outside. (If you're using pins, be careful not to pierce yourself!) Stuff the ears with batting, foam, or small snips of scrap fabric until they look full. The eraser end of a pencil is a very effective tool for tamping and stuffing.

6 Place a staple or a few stitches along the open edge (do not use pins), or just leave the bottom open. Fold the fabric on the open edge slightly up into the ear to create a flat or slightly concave bottom. While looking in a mirror, position the ears on your head and secure at the corners using bobby pins.

ADJUSTING

Now, remove the ears, unstuff them, and turn them inside out again. This is the time to make any changes or adjustments. Are the ears the right size? Do you want to make them bigger or smaller? Fix anything about the shape?

If you need to make changes, use a staple puller to remove the staples, adjust, and restaple as needed. Or, make a new tracing and then a new muslin test pair until you have exactly what you want.

Once you're happy with the result, trace along the staple or pin lines with a pen or pencil (pencil is best if you're working with thin fabric, to avoid ink "bleed-through"). Remove all of the staples and place tracing paper over each piece of material. Make a new template by tracing over the drawn lines and around the edges of the material.

Once you're happy with your test pair, and have retraced your pattern onto a new piece of tracing paper, you have your final pattern. Now you're ready to start working with the fabric of your choice for your final costume.

FINISHING

Using your good material, follow steps 1 through 3. Then, instead of stapling or pinning the fabric together in step 4, sew the pairs together along the sewing line with a needle and thread (leave the bottom open). Now turn your ears right side out so the finished side is on the outside, stuff them, tuck in the bottom, and sew them closed.

Fabric on the Cheap When picking out your final fabric, you'll no doubt want to find exactly the right color and finish, but that doesn't necessarily mean you have to pay top dollar for it. The remnant or scrap bin at the fabric store—typically, a little cart, box, or bin where all the leftover bits and pieces of fabric from longer rolls or bolts are stored—is a great source for quality fabric priced at a fraction of the material's original retail price. Since ears and even tails can be created with less than a full yard of material, remnants are usually more than big enough to complete an entire project. If you're willing to spend a little time digging through the scrap pile, you might find exactly what you need.

STEP BY STEP

LESS BASIC CAT EARS

Now that you've made a very basic set of ears, let's try something a bit more complex. Instead of an ear all in one color, with the same fabric for both the inside and the outside, a more realistic cat's ear would have a furry outside and a pink inside. These are the "pinna"—anatomically speaking, all cats have an exterior pinna and an interior pinna, the outside and inside "flaps" of the ears.

The step-by-step instructions here are for a finished set of ears, but it is highly recommended that you make a muslin test first before cutting into your final fabric.

This is a pattern for a basic ear inset to go with your basic ear pattern. Trace this pattern onto a piece of tracing paper and carefully cut out the tracing along the solid lines.

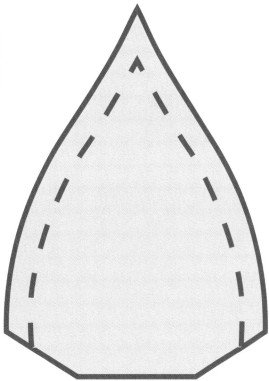

1 Using your chosen fabric for the outsides of the ears, follow steps 1 through 3 of BASIC CAT EARS. You will have 2 pairs of material, with lines already drawn to mark where the fabric will be sewn together. Repeat the same process using the basic ear inset pattern, using pink fabric for the insides of the ears. You will only need 2 pieces of this material instead of 4.

HINT You have 2 templates now—a large one, for the outsides of the ears, and a small one, for the insets. If you lay the inset template on top of the basic ear shape, you can get a preview of what the finished ear will look like. Make your adjustments at this stage, for a larger or smaller inset.

Basic Ear swatches

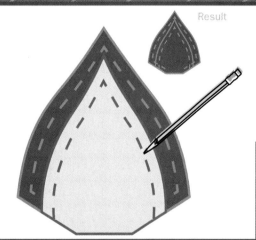
Result

2 Take 1 piece of fabric from each pair of "outside" ears. (Not the pink inset fabric.) Trace all lines from the inset pattern onto the "rough" side of the fabric. These will be the "fronts" of the ears. Set the other pieces aside. They will be the ear backs.

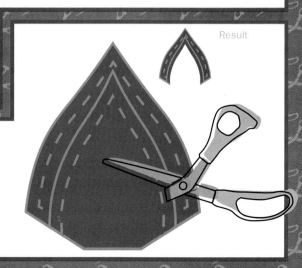
Result

3 Carefully cut windows in the 2 ear pieces along the new inner lines. The outside lines are your sewing guidelines.

4 Pair these pieces up with the pink insert pieces, making sure that the rough sides of both pieces are facing the same direction.

Result

HINT If you don't feel up to this much fussy sewing, an extremely easy way to get the effect of an inset is to hot-glue a piece of pink satin or felt on the front side of a simple pair of ears. It's not a perfect method—the edges of the inset will show, especially on very furry fabric, but it's fine for a quick and easy pair of ears.

Result

5 Pin or staple the 2 pieces of material together. (Fold back the fabric edges toward the "rough" side to sew.) Visually inspect each piece before final sewing to make sure that the inset lays smooth and that all the seam edges are concealed. If the pieces don't fit together perfectly, pull the pins or staples, and adjust your patterns. When the fit is just right, sew the inserts into place along the guidelines.

6 Now, take the set-aside fabric pieces for the ear backs and match them up to your new inset ear pieces (rough sides out). Sew the fronts to the backs, turn right side out, stuff, and finish just as you did in BASIC CAT EARS.

EAR ATTACHMENTS

There are a number of ways to attach ears to your head. Basic cat ears can be held on easily with hairpins (as long as they're not too big). Combs are also a good choice for supporting most styles of ears, but heavier, longer, or larger ears will require the more solid support of a headband. An inexpensive headband from the drugstore works just fine for this purpose, although you can also find more elaborate fabric headbands in bridal or sewing departments (these can at least save you a decision about whether or not to cover your headband with fabric). If you want to cover your headband with a custom fabric, one easy method is to attach your ears directly to the fabric, and then hot-glue the fabric to the headband. Of course, all this can also be sewn.

USING COMBS

1 Measure your ear pattern across the base. You'll want a comb that's a little smaller than this measurement. You can also cut down a larger comb using a hobby saw or even a pair of heavy shears.

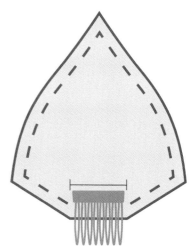

2 Follow steps 1 through 4 of BASIC CAT EARS. Turn the fabric right side out, but do not stuff or sew the ears closed yet. Place the comb onto the excess material at the bottom of the ear, between the two pieces of material.

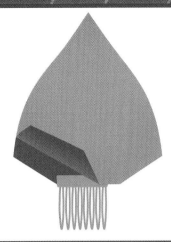

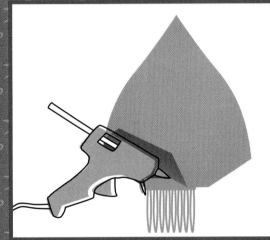

3 Hot-glue or sew the comb into place using strong or monofilament thread. Attach the comb to one side of the fabric only—leave the other piece of material loose.

4 Stuff the ears as normal. Now, close the ear at the bottom by stitching the free flap of material to its partner on the other side. The comb should now be firmly located between the two pieces.

USING A HEADBAND

1 If you want to cover your headband with fabric, measure the headband along the curve from one end to the other. This is the length. Now measure across the narrow direction. Pull out your calculator and multiply this number by 2.2. This will be the pattern width.

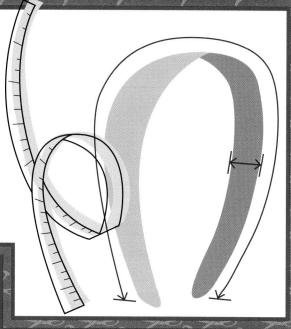

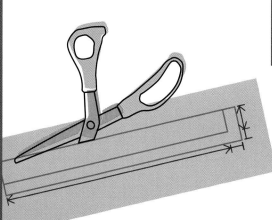

2 Cut a piece of muslin or other material for prototyping ½ inch longer and ½ inch wider than the headband measurements obtained in step one.

HINT Place the seam where the material will be sewn along the underside of the band so that it won't show when you're finished.

3 Fold the material in half along the length, finished side out. Staple or pin about ¼ inch in from the sides along the length to make a fabric tube. (This seam will be hidden underneath the headband, so don't worry about turning the fabric inside-out to sew.) Slide your headband into the tube. If it is too tight or loose, adjust the pins or staples accordingly, and mark the material.

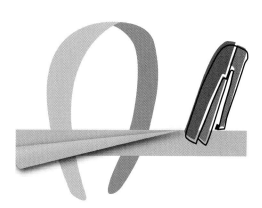

4 Once you have your prototype fitted, take out the staples or pins and lay the material flat. With a pair of BASIC CAT EARS (steps 1 through 6, stuffed and closed), locate where you wish the ears to be on the headband and mark the material. Make sure to mark where the ears will start and end. Transfer all markings onto tracing paper.

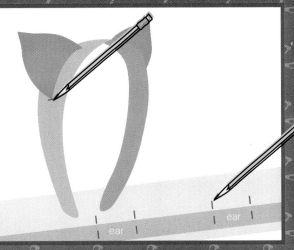

5 Now, using the paper pattern, transfer all markings to the finished side of your good material. Stitch your finished ears to the material in the positions you've marked.

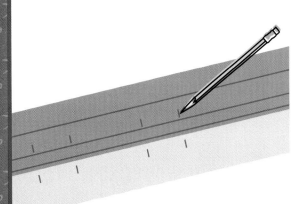

6 Next, stitch the headband cover itself closed along its length. Slide your headband into the cover, and close the ends.

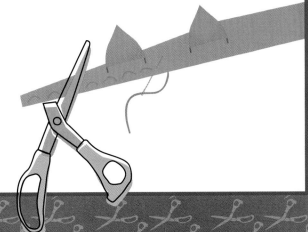

CUSTOMIZING

Now that you have a basic grasp on how to make catgirl ears, start thinking about how you can change them or add to them. How can you alter the basic shape of the ears to make them your own? What different types of materials can you use that would change the ears? Cosplay is a never-ending process of finding and creating new and different ways to make your visions a reality. Let your own creativity guide you!

Tuck ears behind a visor.

Ears sewn directly to a hat can be taken off at a moment's notice.

A hood lets you hide reinforcements and seams under fabric.

Hoods Headbands and combs are only two ways of wearing cat ears. There are many ways to attach ears to your costume—such as attaching them directly to your costume! If your outfit has some kind of headgear, such as a hat or a hood, you can stitch or glue the ears directly to that. A plus to this treatment is that you can put on and take off your ears in a hurry if you need to without fussing with adjusting pins, combs, or headbands.

Ears attached to a headband.

These ears are attached to the goggles.

A headdress can support even heavy ears.

Thick hair can cover up a headband or combs.

A headband holds these ears in a listening pose.

Wire-supported bunny ears need to be as light as you can make them so they'll stand up!

STEP BY STEP

BASIC CAT TAILS

For a more complete catgirl costume, you'll definitely want a tail. Tails are a little more complicated than ears—unlike ears, which are generally one-size-fits-all, tails must be adjusted to your height. No matter how attractive it might seem to have a tail long enough to drag on the floor, it's no fun to be wearing something that you'll be constantly stepping on or tripping over!

The easiest way to scale out the length of your tail is to measure it against your body. Pin or hold the fabric you plan to use against the spot on your body where your tail will eventually be attached, and measure out the material to the length you want. Do you want the tail to fall above your knees, or below? Make a mark with a pen or pencil wherever you want your tail to end. Remember to leave a little extra to allow for the fabric taken up by sewing.

STARTER MATERIALS

- inexpensive muslin fabric (available at fabric stores) or other scrap test fabric, about 1 yard
- pencil, fine-tip marker, or ballpoint pen
- tracing paper or tissue paper or white gift-wrapping paper
- scissors
- straight pins or hand stapler and staples
- ruler or tape measure
- cotton batting or foam pillow stuffing
- sewing needle and thread
- calculator
- wire (from a craft store) or a wire coat hanger
- wire cutters
- needle-nose pliers

1 Do your calculations for length and width. Then, mark out those measurements on a piece of your tracing paper. Essentially, you'll have a pair of straight parallel lines. These are the sewing lines, where you'll be joining the material together to make a tube.

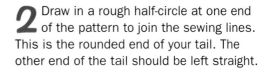

HINT You can, of course, make your tail pattern to the exact width and length you want, but practically speaking, the width is the only part of the tail pattern that really matters. A short pattern piece can be used to mark out a single piece of fabric to any length—just move the pattern piece along the fabric, using a yardstick or other straight edge, in a straight line, until the tail is the length you want. This way, you can make any number of tail lengths from a single pattern.

2 Draw in a rough half-circle at one end of the pattern to join the sewing lines. This is the rounded end of your tail. The other end of the tail should be left straight.

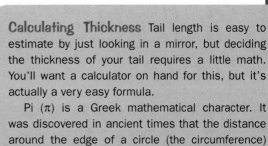

Calculating Thickness Tail length is easy to estimate by just looking in a mirror, but deciding the thickness of your tail requires a little math. You'll want a calculator on hand for this, but it's actually a very easy formula.

Pi (π) is a Greek mathematical character. It was discovered in ancient times that the distance around the edge of a circle (the circumference) divided by its diameter (the distance across) is the same for any circle. Since a tail is essentially a long tube, the fabric forms a circle. So pi can be used to tell you how much fabric you'll need to create the precise thickness of your tail.

If you want your tail, say 2 inches thick, multiply that number by pi. (Many calculators have a key for pi. If yours doesn't, enter 3.14 instead.) The answer is approximately 6.28, or about 6¼ inches. This is the width of fabric you'll need to make a tail that's 2 inches wide. Again, remember to cut the fabric a little larger to leave room for the material taken up when you sew it together.

3 Measure ¼ inch outside each line you've drawn and draw a second pair of lines. Extend the lines to your desired length. Then cut out your pattern along the outside lines, and transfer the markings to the "rough" side of your fabric. Cut out the material along the outside lines. You should end up with a long strip of fabric with a single rounded end.

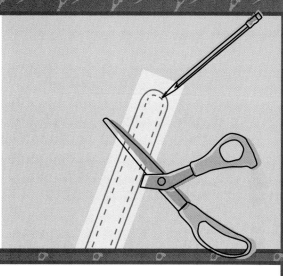

HINT Remember to leave a little extra room for attaching your tail to your costume—an extra 2 inches, at least. If you have too much material, you can always trim the excess away.

4 Fold the material in half, pairing up the sewing lines. Sew or staple closed along the lines.

5 Turn the tail right side out and stuff with cotton batting or other soft stuffing material.

HINT When stuffing a full-length tail, it is far easier to stuff the tail as you are turning it right side out rather than trying to cram stuffing all the way down the full length of the tail. The trick is rather like putting on a nylon stocking—put in your stuffing and pack it down carefully as you roll the material down until you've reached the end.

MAKING YOUR TAIL POSABLE

1 Create a tail as described in the BASIC CAT TAIL instructions, but don't turn it right side out or stuff it just yet.

HINT There are several ways to make a tail so that it will hold its shape. The easiest method is to use wire. You can buy spooled wire for this purpose at a hardware store, but a basic wire coat hanger works just fine too, and the only real difference in the assembly process is in how you go about stuffing your tail to include the wire. Using a pair of pliers, untwist and straighten out the neck of a hanger, then cut it just below the twisted part; now you have about 33 inches of wire ready to use, just about enough for a 30-inch tail.

2 Cut the length of wire you need with needle-nose pliers (or, if the wire is heavy, use wirecutters). Twist a loop in each end of the wire with pliers so there's no sharp end to poke through your tail once it's fully assembled.

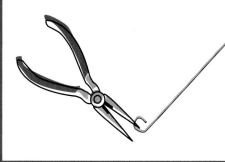

3 To stuff your tail: pack some material into the tip of the tail and place one end of the wire onto the tail stuffing. Fold some of the stuffing around the wire—you want the wire to be in the center. Then, "roll" the tail over the stuffing and wire as you would put on a pair of pantyhose or a knee sock until you've reached the end of the tail.

ATTACHING YOUR TAIL

How to go about attaching your tail depends largely on the rest of your costume. If you want your tail to be a permanent part of your costume, simply close off the end of the tail and sew it wherever you'd like it to be on the inside or outside of the garment. If you are planning to wear your tail over a belt, stuff and sew the end of the tail closed and then cut two slits in the sides of the tail to accomodate the belt. Remove any stuffing in that section and thread the belt through. If you are using wire in your tail, make sure the tail is on the outside of the belt for comfort reasons.

Tails can be worn with anything—skirts, jeans, or even leotards, although a wire-reinforced tail might be too heavy to be attached to a thin material like spandex. Be sure to keep the tail's weight in mind when designing your costume—if it's too heavy, it will not only be uncomfortable, but it will drag and distort the line of your outfit, or even tear thin material. This is really something to keep in mind when wearing a tights-and-leotard outfit!

Another thing to remember when attaching a tail is that if the tail should happen to get pulled on or down (either on purpose or by getting caught in an elevator door for example), whatever the tail is attached to might also get pulled down with it. If you plan on wearing a tail with a skirt or dress, consider wearing a belt under your skirt with the tail attached to it. This can simply be a strip of material with hook-and-loop fastenings (Velcro®) on the ends.

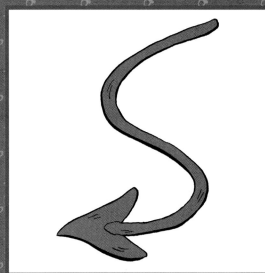

A simple devil tail from a Halloween store can be easily adapted into a cat or other critter tail.

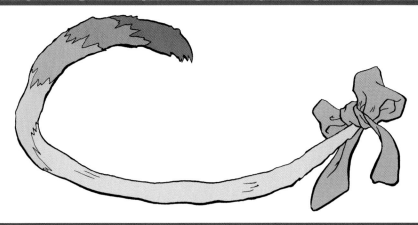

You can make a Siamese cat tail by darkening the color of the fur toward the tip.

A simple tail with bells.

Adding a puffball to the end of a simple tail changes a cat to a lion.

A simple puffball of fur fabric makes a bunny's cottontail.

This brushy tiger tail will need lots of stuffing to make it look fierce!

This wolf's tail is reinforced with wire to create a graceful downward curve.

A spotted leopard's tail with a brushy, darkened tip.

BASIC CAT PAWS

Paws are the final addition to a catgirl costume. The most common type of paw is basically a mitten, and the disadvantage of wearing paws is the same as wearing mittens. You have no individual finger movement, so there are things you can't do with your hands in a finished costume. While this isn't a worry for catgirls who only exist in manga, anime, or games, it can be an annoying limitation for cosplayers, especially if you're planning on spending a full day in costume.

As always, we recommend making a muslin prototype of your paw design before cutting into your good material.

1 Place your hand on a piece of paper and roughly trace it in mitten form. Then, draw a line about ½ inch outside of that. This will be the sewing line. Then, draw a line about ¼ inch outside of that. Cut out along this line. This will be the pattern for your mitten liner.

HINT Make sure to leave the opening for your wrist wide enough to get your hand in and out of the mitten.

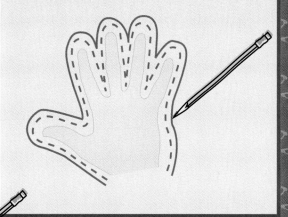

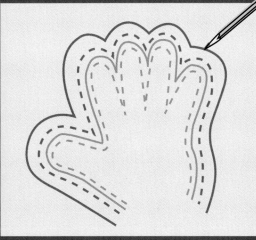

2 Take the pattern for your liner and trace the outside lines onto another sheet of paper. Next, add another line about ¼ inch outside of that. This will be your sewing line. Now add another line ½ inch outside of that. Cut out along this line. This is the outside paw pattern.

HINT Remember that you'll need a right-hand paw and a left-hand paw—make 1 set of fabric pairs with the pattern facing one way, then turn the pattern over to make a mirror-image version.

3 Carefully cut out the pieces along the outside lines, making your initial cuts just a little bigger than the rough line you've drawn. Separate the material into 2 pairs, arrange the pairs with the finished sides facing each other, "rough" sides facing out. Remember, the liner pieces will not show, so you can make them out of muslin or other inexpensive fabric.

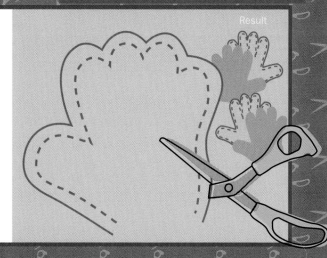

Result

4 Match up the fabric pieces for the outside mitten with the rough side of the fabric facing out. Sew the 2 mitten pieces together along the sewing line, leaving the wrist open. Turn the mitten inside out. The finished side of the fabric should now be on the outside. Repeat with the mitten liner, only you'll want the smooth surface on the inside, next to your hand. You should have 2 finished mittens now, one smaller than the other.

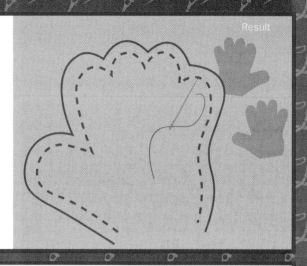

Result

5 Slip the mitten liner onto your hand. Then slide the outside paw glove on over it. Add foam, batting, or other stuffing to fill up the gap between the 2 paws.

6 With the liner inside the stuffed outside paw, fold over the open wrist of the outside paw and sew it to the inside cuff of the liner. Repeat the process for the second paw.

MORE REALISTIC PAWS

Real cats don't just have mittens for paws, of course, they have fingers, and it's easy to add the illusion of cat fingers to your paw design. When outlining your pattern, add lines in the rough shape of oversized fingers. Then, before you sew the mittens together, pinch the material together along each finger line and sew a seam down the length of each line. Turn the mitten right side out and continue as before. The stuffing will fill out the finger shapes and help create the illusion of cat fingers.

If you want your cat to have claws, small press-on plastic fingernails slipped through the paw seams and hot-glued firmly in place are one easy trick for a clawlike effect. However, you might want to think carefully before incorporating sharp claws into your design, as many conventions have regulations about costume weapons, and if your claws are sharp enough, they could possibly be prohibited. You don't want to have to leave off a part of your costume because it's deemed too dangerous to be worn in the halls! A better alternative is small pieces of white felt folded over into a cone shape and sewn or glued onto the ends of the paws for decorative claws that won't scratch.

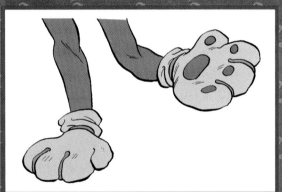

Cartoony paws based on mittens.

Realistic paws attached to wristbands.

Fangs and fingered paws make the most detailed catgirl.

Cat Fangs Catgirls in anime and manga typically have fangs—cute, snaggly little fangs rather like vampire teeth, drawn protruding slightly from under a girl's upper lip. Actually creating your own set of custom teeth is a bit outside the scope of this book, but if you desire a pair of catlike fangs, practically any costume shop, Halloween store, or novelty store carries some type of inexpensive plastic fangs that can be held into place with a special putty or dental glue. Try out a few different types until you find one that fits the look you want.

MAKING YOUR COSTUME COMPLETE

Once you have ears, a tail, and paws, what else is there? Well, the whole rest of your costume, of course. What you want to wear with your catgirl ears, tail, and paws is totally up to you—you can just add them onto your normal street clothes, and presto, a casual catgirl.

Or, you can create an entire persona for your catgirl alter ego, with a leotard and tights, or a frilly dress, or wherever your imagination takes you. Or, you could replicate an existing anime, manga, or game character, which we'll be discussing in Part Three.

A simple leotard can be dressed up with fur sleeves and leggings.

Don't forget about props! A rose for an elegant character.

A Chinese dress and fan completes this Siamese catgirl.

An elaborate dress will catch attention.

Express your character's attitude by paying attention to details.

Put a bell on this mischievous cat.

This catgirl's ready for an island adventure.

Note the tail attached to this festival girl's kimono.

Simple schoolgirl with cat ears and tail.

A witchy black magic cat (don't try flying at home!).

Martial arts catgirls kick butt.

A schoolgirl cat running late for class!

two

Creating Other Critters

Catgirls are certainly the most common type of critter you'll run across, but there are plenty more to be found in cosplay. Most other critters, however, have a lot in common with the venerable catgirl. Ears, a tail, paws—once you know how to make the cat versions, modifying the designs for different critters is a snap. All it takes is a little imagination. Keep an open mind, let your creativity lead you, and you'll find yourself up to your paws in critter costumes in no time.

MODIFYING EARS

No matter what kind of critter you want to cosplay as, ears are still basically ears. The only real difference in making ears for different animals is their shapes. A lion will have round ears instead of pointed ones. A mouse also has round ears, but larger (proportionally) than a lion's. A rabbit has taller and thinner ears. These differences typically lead to a more complicated construction. A catgirl's short ears can stand up easily, but a tall set of bunny ears or a mouse's large, round ears will droop seriously without some extra structure to make them hold their shape.

There are two major solutions to this problem: build a wire frame to support the ear, much like the wire in catgirl tails, or create a stiff insert out of rigid material such as Styrofoam, foam board, cardboard, or plastic. Both methods have their advantages.

Bending Wire Floral wire can be bent with your fingers, but solid-core wire may need the help of a pair of fine-nose pliers to give you extra leverage. When working with wire, it doesn't hurt to wear a pair of work or gardening gloves to protect your hands from accidental jabs.

WIRE FRAMES

When using wire, there are a couple of things you need to consider. The first is weight—you always want your ears to be as light as possible. A too-heavy pair of ears will be hard to keep on your head without sliding off. Remember, all that's holding your ears on in most cases is a headband or pins! Too much weight also means a lot of stress on your neck and shoulders. You don't want to end up with something that'll be too uncomfortable to wear for long periods, such as the several hours you'd spend at the average cosplay competition!

STARTER MATERIALS

- floral wire or solid-core wire, 16 or 22 gauge, about 2 ft.
- wire cutters
- needle-nose pliers
- hot glue (optional)
- work gloves or gardening gloves (optional)

HINT Wire is, in general, fairly inexpensive and most often sold by the foot. Floral wire, available at almost any craft or fabric store, is a good choice for lightweight ears such as rabbit ears. For shapes that require more strength, take a trip to your local hardware store and ask a salesperson to help you find solid-core wire (one strand of metal wire rather than many thinner ones). You will most likely be asked what "gauge" (thickness) you will need. It is a good idea in the beginning to try at least a couple of different sizes, such as 16 or 22, so you can compare differences in strength.

1 After you've made your prototype ears, but before you turn them right-side out and stuff them, take a piece of wire and "trace" an ear, bending the wire to match the ear's shape. Make sure to make this outline a little smaller than the ear itself, because the frame you're making will have to fit inside the ear. Try to make the wire shape fit just inside the sewing or staple line. Leave a few extra inches of wire at both ends of the frame.

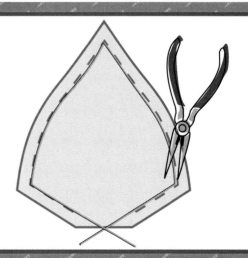

2 Cut the wire. You can hot-glue the wire into place at the tips or sew it in place with a couple of quick stitches around the top of the wire.

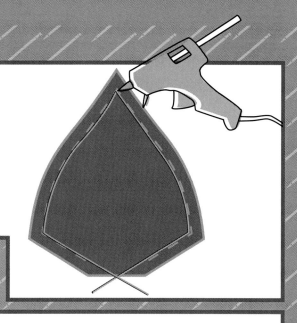

3 Turn the ear right-side out and slide it over the wire, like putting on a sock. Stuff as usual and sew closed at the bottom, leaving the wire ends protruding. Bend loops into the end of the wire so there are no sharp ends.

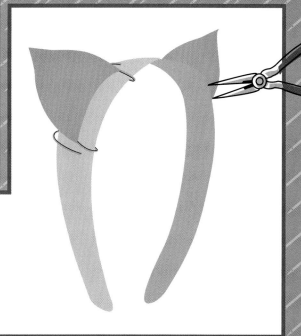

4 Position your ears over the headband or combs you'll be using for support. Cover with fabric (or not) as normal. Glue or twist the ends of the wire around the headband or combs to hold the ear in place.

BOARD SUPPORTS

You can also make a hard support from a rigid material such as foam board or very thin plastic. Like a wire frame, a board support is simply a cutout in the shape of the ear, a little smaller so as to fit inside the ear, and a little longer than the fabric ear itself. As with wires, use the lightest material you can find that will still hold its shape at the size you need. If the form is too heavy, the ears will fall over.

STARTER MATERIALS

- foam board or other light Styrofoam board or thin plastic matting, about a 12-inch square
- heavy scissors or utility knife
- pen or pencil
- hot glue
- work gloves or gardening gloves (optional)

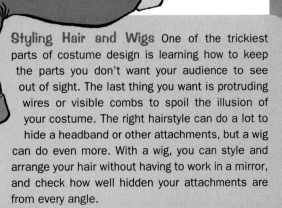

Styling Hair and Wigs One of the trickiest parts of costume design is learning how to keep the parts you don't want your audience to see out of sight. The last thing you want is protruding wires or visible combs to spoil the illusion of your costume. The right hairstyle can do a lot to hide a headband or other attachments, but a wig can do even more. With a wig, you can style and arrange your hair without having to work in a mirror, and check how well hidden your attachments are from every angle.

1 Trace the shape of the ear on the board with a pen or pencil and cut it out with heavy scissors or a utility knife.

HINT Be very careful when using a knife, making sure to never cut directly toward yourself and keeping your fingers tucked under, out of the cutting line. A knife can skid very easily on foam board or plastic if you're not careful! If you're at all uncomfortable with handling a knife, use a heavy pair of scissors to make your cuts.

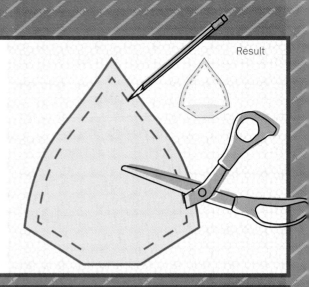

Result

2 Hot-glue the board into place (probably at the tip of the ear will be enough) before stuffing the ears. Unroll the ear over the board like a sock so that it ends up right-side out with the board inside. Place stuffing on both sides of the board so the ear won't have a "flat" appearance on one side.

3 Glue the bottom edge of the board to your headband or comb before closing off the fabric, so the ear won't flop loosely back and forth.

MODIFYING TAILS

A bunny has a puffy tail, a squirrel has a bushy one, and a lion has a tail that looks much like a catgirl's except for the addition of a tuft of fur at the end. But whatever kind of tail you might be creating, there are a few pieces of good advice that apply to all.

Wire can be used in tails much as the coat hanger in BASIC CAT TAILS, or even like the wire frames for ears if the tail is a smaller and unusual shape. The process is basically the same for either. Be careful not to make your tail too big or too heavy, or it will be hard to attach and support on your costume without drooping.

As always, making a prototype for unusual tail shapes is strongly recommended. It's far better to work out the design at the prototype stage than waste good fabric on a faulty design. Never assume, for example, that you can just take two circles and sew them together to make a ball-like tail. It won't work. In the prototype stage, however, you can use inexpensive materials, and add or remove fabric until you get the tail just how you like it. It may take several tries before you get the exact result that you want.

If you get stuck trying to figure out how to create a particular effect, look around for other items that are shaped like what you want, and study how they're put together. Is your desired tail round and tapered to a point? Look at how a football is put together. Is it round like a ball? Maybe a beach ball would offer a hint to help you. You will likely find that whatever you

are making, someone has made something with a similar shape. Seek out these things and make it your mission to see all of the things the world has to offer from the perspective of a cosplayer. If you're open to observing the world, the secrets of creating new shapes will open up to you.

MATCHING FUR

Matching fur, either to create the effect of a "real" animal's fur or the artificial look of a fictional character, can be difficult. While there are many manufacturers of fake fabric fur on the market, and many different styles, there's no guarantee that the character you're hoping to portray will be represented by one of them. Often you can come close with a purchased fabric, but rarely can you get an exact match.

Creating custom-dyed fur is a bit beyond what we can do in this book, but there are a number of methods you can use to come up with a good match.

If the fur you want has stripes or spots, take a prototype section of your costume with you to where you shop for fur—an ear or a paw. Mark your prototype with the pattern you're hoping to find. Use those markings as a guide to size and spacing to help you find the fur that best matches what you're looking for. Look for things such as the number of stripes across the back of the paw, or how large or numerous the spots are.

For solid colors, take a color photo or printout to match against fabric colors. It still doesn't hurt to have a prototype ear or tail on hand to help you try to match things such as the length and texture of the fur, and also to judge the thickness of the fabric.

CUSTOM COLORING FUR

Although fake furs can be found in almost any color or pattern you can imagine, sometimes your chosen character's fur will have an effect that you simply must do for yourself, such as "gradation," a light or dark change of color toward the ends of the fur. There are simple techniques to match this effect. Always test your technique on a scrap piece of fur first to get an idea of how well the fur will take color; after you have mastered the technique on a scrap piece, you can use the same process using fabric or acrylic paints.

Aside from the paints themselves, the materials you'll need for this are easy to find and inexpensive: an old hairbrush, an old toothbrush, fabric scraps to use as rags, and a blow dryer. Custom brushes can be made by trimming off excess bristles to create the best tool for your specific job.

STARTER MATERIALS

- an old or disposable hairbrush or toothbrush
- watercolor, tempera, or other water-based paint (for test version)
- fabric or acrylic paint (for final version)
- cloth rags (nothing that you'll be worried about staining)
- water
- blow dryer

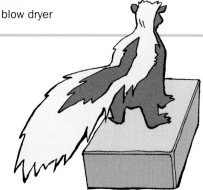

Choosing Fabric You should, if possible, shop around to find as close a match as possible; keeping in mind that some things, such as the exact "furriness" or the number of stripes or spots, are not likely to ever be matched perfectly. There are, after all, some compromises that have to be made when transforming two-dimensional characters into a three-dimensional world. But when you do find a material you like, be sure to buy enough of it to finish your whole costume, if not a little extra. Fabrics, like clothes, go in and out of fashion, and the last thing you want is to run out of material and find yourself trying to replace a discontinued piece of fabric! You might have to repurchase new material all over again, just so that everything matches.

1 Using watercolor, tempera, or another easily removable, water-based paint, take up some of the color in a wet cloth and gently "pet" a scrap piece of fur with the cloth. Make sure the cloth is only slightly damp and not dripping wet. (While latex paint is not suggested, if you want to use it, make sure that it is well thinned with water.)

2 Using a hairbrush, brush the fur in the direction of the fur "growth" to separate the strands and to disperse the color. Be careful not to oversaturate the fur or the color will blob or clump together.

3 Gently "pet" the fur with a dry cloth to remove excess color. Air dry or gently blow dry. (If you blow dry, be careful not to overheat the fur!) Then, with a dry brush, gently rebrush the fur in the opposite direction to separate any strands that have become stuck together.

HINT Compare the fur against your character art. Repeat the process to add more color if needed. You will get better results by doing the color in multiple layers than trying to do it all at once.

STRIPES OR SPOTS ON FUR

Just as with faux fur in custom colors, many varieties of striped and spotted fur fabrics can be found for sale, but these tend to be quite expensive. If your chosen character has striped or spotted fur, here's how to replicate these features on the cheap.

STARTER MATERIALS

- an old or disposable hairbrush or toothbrush
- watercolor, tempera, or other water-based paint (for test version)
- fabric or acrylic paint (for final version)
- cloth rags (nothing that you'll be worried about staining)
- tailor's chalk (found at fabric stores)
- water
- blow dryer

1 With a scrap piece of fur, mark out your desired stripes or spots using a piece of tailor's chalk (or the sharp edge of a regular piece of chalk). Then, pull the fur back in the reverse direction of the fur "growth," making the hairs more or less stand up. Be careful not to rub away the chalk marks!

2 Start at the end of your marked area. Using an old toothbrush soaked with color, brush the fur from the base of the hairs toward the tips. Repeat this process in small sections until you have done all of the fur in your marked area. Apply the color sparingly—too much color will make the fur clump. For bright colors, build up the paint in layers.

3 Gently "pet" the fur with a dry cloth to remove excess color. Air dry or gently blow dry. Be careful not to overheat the fur.

4 Using a hairbrush, brush the dried fur to separate the hairs and to fluff it back out. Be careful to make sure the color is dry before doing this or you may spread color from the brush to other areas of the fur you hadn't intended to color.

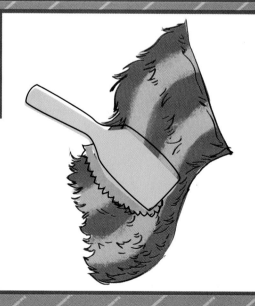

Take me out . . . . This baseball bunny's ears are attached to her batting helmet.

A mouse? A ninja? A ninja mouse!

Monkey see, monkey do, Monkey King! Note traditional tiger pelt around waist.

This foxy girl has a lot of tails! Be sure you can support all that weight before trying the nine-tailed fox.

Little Red Riding Hood meets the Big Bad Wolf.

Think how you could make this Halloween devil girl into a cat with a little costume conversion.

Black and white fur fabric makes a perfect panda girl.

A rabbit from a hat? Or a rabbit with a hat? Both!

This cute cowgirl's really a pony.

Accessories such as swords should be checked with con security.

A heavy tail like this squirrel's might be hard to support.

A mouse girl with a Gothic flavor.

Fruit Bat Lass's wings are framed with wire.

Nurse Skunk's tail is attached to her belt.

Speedy roller skates for a kangaroo rat.

three

Duplicating Characters

To many cosplayers, the real challenge of cosplay is duplicating an established character from a popular manga, anime, or game right down to the last, painstaking detail. This can be an expression of love for a favorite character, a way to draw more attention to your costume by portraying someone everyone will recognize, or simply a display of your costume construction skill in competition, as very few character designers bother to make sure their designs are easy to replicate in reality!

CHOOSING A CHARACTER

If you're interested in duplicating a character, odds are good that you already have a character picked out, someone that you particularly like from a show you watch, a game you play, or a manga that's earned a special spot in your heart. A really successful duplication, though, isn't just a matter of recreating a costume.

The first thing you need to take into account in picking a character to cosplay is your own body type and appearance. It almost goes without saying that the most accurate recreations tend to be characters that match your own size, shape, or coloring the best. For example, a little girl character is easier to recreate for a short person than a tall one.

However, attitude is also a factor. A successful character copy is as much a question of personality as look. How does your personality fit the character you want to cosplay as? Think about characters not only in terms of how they appear, but how they act. The right attitude, combined with attention to costume detail, can override huge differences in physical appearances. Is your character energetic and bouncy? Dignified and quiet? Sophisticated and elegant? Insights such as these will help you to make a good match for yourself that won't force you to put on any kind of "act" to make the character come alive. Then, if you decide to participate in cosplay competitions, you will already be ahead of the game on performance!

The Combination Catgirl Anime-style catgirls are not, strictly speaking, cats. This is an important distinction. They're also not, in most cases, simply people wearing cat costumes, à la Catwoman from the *Batman* comics or movies. A better comparison would be a *Playboy*-style bunny girl—the bunny aspects are only the final, finishing touch to an outfit that is largely about being a sexy girl. But an anime, manga, or game catgirl is even more than that. They are characters first, often multilayered ones, plus they have cat features. The cat is only the topmost layer to any number of possible characters: kung fu girls, space girls, gothic girls, schoolgirls—all can be catgirls, every one unique!

CATGIRL CHARACTERS AND TYPES

Catgirl characters are so numerous in anime, manga, and games that a complete list of them would be next to impossible! However, in the interest of giving you a starter list of catgirl characters to choose from, we present a sample few. Look around, though—there are plenty more to choose from!

SOME POPULAR CATGIRLS

This is only a small sampling of the characters to be found in anime and games.

Character	Source
Aisha Clan-Clan	*Outlaw Star*
Annapuma and Yumipuma / The Puma Twins	*Dominion: Tank Police*
Atsuko Natsume / Nuku Nuku	*All Purpose Cultural Cat Girl Nuku*
Chesire	*Miyuki-Chan in Wonderland*
Chinami and Yuriko	*Mao-chan*
Dejiko	*Di Gi Charat*
Fam	*Ruin Explorers*
Felicia	*Darkstalkers / Night Warriors*
Ichigo Momomiya / Zoey Hanson	*Tokyo Mew Mew / Mew Mew Power*
Kizna Towryk	*Pilot Candidate*
Maya	*Geobreeders*
Merle	*The Vision of Escaflowne*
Misha and Koboshi	*Pita Ten*
Nariya and Eriya	*The Vision of Escaflowne*
Natsuki	*Hyper Police*
Nyako and Konyako	*Eden's Bowy*
Pink	*Dragon Pink*
Puchiko	*Di Gi Charat*
Sera	*Sonic the Hedgehog*
Shader	*Chrono Crusade*
Tabby	*.hack//ROOTS*
Taruto	*Magical Nyan Nyan Taruto*
The Mithra	*Final Fantasy XI*
Uriko	*Bloody Roar*
Zakuro Fujiwara / Kikki Benjamin	*Tokyo Mew Mew / Mew Mew Power*

VERSIONS AND STAND-ALONES

Even if you already have a character picked out, you'll probably still need to decide which version of the character you want to cosplay as! Nearly any character from a manga, anime, or game has more than one appearance—different costumes, hairstyle variations, or just differences in art styles from game to game or season to season in an anime series. Such slight differences can make for huge variations in the way your costume is put together.

For competition purposes, or just for novelty, some cosplayers enjoy making costumes that have only appeared once in a series, in a single episode or issue. Then, even if other cosplayers pick the same character they did, they're far more likely to stand out from the crowd.

FINDING THE DETAILS

Making a truly great duplicate costume requires attention to details that might otherwise go unnoticed. You might spend many months creating the perfect costume, but most people will have no idea of the dedication and effort that went into it. Other cosplayers and judges, however, will know—they'll be examining practically every square inch of your costume to see how well you've managed to make someone's dreams into a reality.

Movement is one item that you might not think of at first. Does your character have any unusual habits that might affect how the costume should move as well? Try to see your character from the point of view of how he or she might think and act, almost like how an actor might approach a role.

All of this probably sounds like a lot of pressure—and it can be. Some cosplayers place that pressure on themselves to excel, and take the challenge of competition very seriously. But if you simply want to have fun, that's totally fine too—for most cosplayers, the first rule of the game is fun. You will always encounter cosplayers who see their hobby as nothing less than a mission from the gods, as well as those who throw together a makeshift costume the night before a convention, but ultimately, it's up to you to decide how serious or dedicated you want to be.

MATCHING PROPORTIONS

Proportions are the key to good costuming. You might duplicate a costume perfectly, right down to the last detail, but if all the elements are the wrong size compared to your body, the costume won't look "right." So you could say that getting the proportions correct is even more important than matching exact details.

You can get a good start on getting the proportions right before even beginning to build your costume by matching up a photograph of yourself with an image of the character you'd like to create. It's best to work on disposable photocopies of the character artwork and also of your own photograph rather than the originals, so you can sketch and make marks and notes.

Compare the two images. With a pencil or pen, sketch in the cat features on your own body in roughly the same position as they appear in the artwork. How do they look? Think about what you need to adjust to make the two images match. Does the tail need to be thicker? Longer? Shorter? Do the ears need to be bigger or smaller? How about their position on your head?

Finding Character Artwork When looking for reference artwork for your chosen character, you'll want some color images to show you what colors you'll need in making your costume, but artwork that shows you the fine details of an outfit is even more important than color. For the most detailed drawings of your character's outfit, you'll want character design sheets or "line art," the model sheets. These are drawings made by the anime or game character designer to show the animators exactly the same things you'll need for making a costume—pictures of a character, in full detail, from as many different angles as possible. Character design sheets can be found in most anime art books devoted to individual shows, and are also a popular extra on many DVDs. Game line art sometimes shows up in video game magazines, and in art books for games. For manga characters, the manga itself will always be your best guide, although some artists will have color art book collections of their work, especially cover images. Check the resource guide at the back of this book for mail order sources for art books.

MATCHING EARS

While small defects or miscalculation on the ears themselves may slip detection, the size and position of the ears on your head can be easily seen from a distance. Getting the sizes and positioning right is crucial.

ADDING ALL THE ANGLES

One way to figure proportions is with a compass. Take a disposable image of your character's head. (Facing forward is best.) Place the point of a compass (you can find one at a stationery or art supply store) at the center of the face, and draw a circle. You want the circle to just touch the character's chin and the top of their head, or where you think the top of their head is (not the top of the hair!). Then, with a ruler, bisect the face from top to bottom, through the center point, and then from side to side. You'll have a cross in the middle of your character's face, dividing it into four sections.

With these lines, you can now use a protractor (another item from the stationery or art supply store), to measure angles. Place the bottom edge of the protractor

Ears With Attitude Size isn't the only thing that matters when it comes to ears. Position and angle are also important. Think about any other aspects of the ears that set your character apart. You can get most of this from looking at your character art. For example, are your character's ears attached to a headband or ribbon, or are they attached directly to the head? How are the ears positioned in relation to the headband, if there is one? Can you attach the ears to the headband using combs or hairpins? How far back do the ears sit on the character's head? Do your character's ears change position from time to time, depending on mood? If so, which mood will you be using in your finished costume? Or do you want to make your ears posable, with a wire frame, so you can change them during the day?

on the horizontal line you drew. The center point of the protractor (where it's marked 0°) should line up with the spot where you first put the compass, the center of the face. From here, you can draw lines from the face's center to where the cat ears are positioned on the head, and note the angles marked on the protractor.

Then, with a disposable photo of your own face, repeat the same process. Sketch in the positions for the ears using the angles that you obtained above. The size of the ears can be estimated by comparing the marked photo to your reflection in a mirror. With a piece of string or cloth tape measure, find the start and end points for the ears on your head in the photo. This should give you a size for the bottom of the ears, which you can use as a reference for the other dimensions.

But no matter how carefully you measure, your eyes will always be your best guides to making the proportions right. Spend plenty of time on this step until you're sure that you're happy with the size and position of your ears.

The Tail End The final step in the process is to think about your tail in combination with the rest of your costume. Does the tail come out from under a garment, such as a skirt, or does it come out through a garment, such as shorts or jumpsuit? If so, you have to think about the tail's attachment as a major part of its design. Is the character's tail often in contact with some other part of their body, such as curled around an arm or shoulder, and if so, can you attach it there as well, to keep it in place? Finally, does the character's tail change with its mood? If so, do you want to pick a specific mood to portray, or would you rather your tail be adjustable over the course of the day? All these items are factors that can contribute to the design.

MATCHING TAILS

Anime and manga characters often have unreasonably long legs in proportion to the rest of their body. While there is nothing to be done about this (other than wearing platform shoes or boots, a trick that doesn't work for every costume), the best approach to matching tail proportions is to measure the tail length against the part of your body that it will appear next to the most often. Look at the image you plan to use as your example. If the tail is mostly below the waist, keep it in proportion to your legs. If the tail is mostly above the waist, keep it in proportion to the upper body. It is possible to find a happy middle ground, but at the very least, your tail should match one proportion as perfectly as possible.

Matching your tail's proportion as compared to your legs: working with a mirror and comparing yourself to your character art, take note of where the tip of the tail falls, or (if the tail is curled up) where it would fall if it was stretched out. Does it fall mid-calf? Mid-thigh? Measure out this distance on your body with a cloth tape measure, or with a piece of string that you can measure later against a ruler. This is the working length of your tail. Proceed as with the instructions in BASIC CAT TAILS to fine-tune the length as necessary. To calculate the length of the tail in proportion to the upper body, the same process works—think of the tail as stretched out, and note where it would fall against your upper body. Proceed as above.

Designing For Curves Tails rarely hang straight. Most of them have a curve, or at the very least a curl at the end. Matching a tail's curve follows the same rules as matching the proportions for length: look to the body for clues and comparisons. Does the tail curve in closely to the character's head, waist, or other body part?

The next thing that you will want to approach is the thickness of the tail. Find a body part on yourself to compare with that of the character, such as the wrist. If, for example, the character's tail is one-half the thickness of the character's wrist, measure your own wrist and divide that measurement by two. This will at least give you a starting point that you can adjust as necessary during the prototype process.

MATCHING PAWS

Matching paws can possibly be the most difficult task of duplicating a character. Very often the character's paw will not conform directly to the anatomy or range of motion that a cat might have. Luckily, most artists working in anime and manga are more familiar with human anatomy than that of cats, so some comparisons can be made that you can use to recreate a decent set of paws. Again, you will have to use your eye a lot here to make the comparisons, but with a little attention to detail you can pull it off with confidence.

With your character art in hand, study the proportions of the character's arm, from elbow to fingertips, and the length and thickness of the "fingers" to overall paw. Then, measure your own arm and, using the measurement, determine the length of that same paw proportion on you. For example, if your arm is 20 inches long, and the paw covers one-half of the character's forearm, then your paw should be one-half of the length of your arm, or 10 inches long. Make a prototype and try it on, adjust accordingly to get the best match between what will work on a human hand and what will most closely match the proportions of the character.

Putting on Paws As with the other body parts, the key to making sure your paws match is to notice any other details that might affect the design. Do the paws come out of your costume's sleeves? If they do, do they seem to fill the sleeve, or do they seem to simply start where the sleeve stops? Are the cuffs of the sleeves especially large, or otherwise unusual to accommodate the paws? Does the character hold something that might be difficult to grasp while wearing the paws? If so, think about attaching the item to the paws permanently, as part of the costume.

four

Taking the Stage

The cosplay competition is nearly always the single most attended event at any convention. It is not at all uncommon for conventions to run out of seating at these events. For a lot of fans, competing in cosplay competitions is perhaps the ultimate recognition that you have done a good job on your costume. It's a great way not only to earn kudos in the cosplay community but to make a name for yourself with the fans who attend the show.

GETTING READY TO COMPETE

Not all cosplayers feel comfortable being onstage in front of hundreds or even thousands of clapping, cheering fans, but assuming that you're ready to take that step, there are a number of things that can not only help you make the very most of your first shot at stardom but will also help ease your anxiety. If there's one piece of advice that seems to work for everything in life, it's this:

Be prepared!

It may be helpful to think of a cosplay competition as something like a wedding, with yourself as the bride. The day of competition is a day that you need to plan for, especially in terms of time. Think about how much time you'll need to get ready (hair, makeup, final adjustments, calming the butterflies in your stomach) and what you'll need to have on hand to ensure that both you and your costume can be in peak condition at showtime.

TYPES OF COSPLAY COMPETITIONS

The first thing that you'll need to know when preparing to compete is exactly what kind of cosplay competition and judging you'll be facing. Nearly every convention has its own unique rules for competitions, variations on how to sign up and qualify for cosplay, and forbidden items (both in and outside of the competitions), so you absolutely must do your homework before showing up at a convention in costume. Thankfully, nearly all conventions now have such information available online, either as a separate section on cosplay on the convention webpage, or in the forum pages.

Every type of competition has advantages and disadvantages—only you can decide what style you'll feel most comfortable with. You may want to enter a few different types of competitions when you're starting out, just to see what kind works best for you.

Here's a quick guide to most common types of competitions.

Walk-On: The cosplayer takes the stage, poses, and then walks off, like a fashion show. Depending on the competition, you might have to pose once for the audience and then once again for the judges who may be sitting off to the side of the stage and so can't see you straight on.

Skit: Either a single cosplayer or a group performs a short sketch for the audience and judges, then strikes a pose and leaves the stage. Skits usually take one of two forms: a reenactment of a particular scene from an anime or game, or an original comedy sketch poking fun at the traits of some or all of the characters involved.

Straight Judging: The contestants are judged separately, and then allowed to take the stage later solely for the fun of the audience. Cosplayers may to be required to answer questions from the judges about the craftsmanship of their costumes, and to explain the process that went into choosing and creating them.

Hall Cosplay: Cosplayers are typically issued a number to be worn and judged as they wander the corridors or other public areas. The judging might also happen in a room set aside for that purpose, but there is no stage appearance in hallway cosplay.

JUDGING

Cosplay judges have a hard job. When assessing a costume, they consider all sorts of factors that many cosplayers wouldn't even begin to think of, from quality of construction to violations of the rules, which can be anything from simple dress codes to limits regarding props. Be aware that almost all conventions have strict rules about props, es-

pecially weapons such as swords, staffs, or very realistic-looking firearms.

Many conventions now do some sort of prejudging, in which the judges (who may or may not be the same judges as for the actual competition) look you over, make sure that you have everything that you are supposed to have (such as source material), and then place you in an appropriate category. Other times, the judges will be eliminating all but the best cosplayers for the competition. If you're disqualified at this stage, don't take it to heart—competition is fierce in a large show, many cosplayers have been at this for years, and the prejudges will sometimes be very experienced cosplayers who have gotten good enough to do costume work for films!

Some conventions judge the contestants separately, even before the actual show, and then let the contestants take the stage later, strictly for the fun of the audience. In these types of competitions it is not at all unusual for contestants to have to answer questions from the judges about the craftsmanship of their costumes. This type of competition is most likely to recognize and credit a truly excellent tailoring job and to include a special award for best craftsmanship.

Audience Participation For a cosplayer on stage, a competition is a unique experience, one you might wish could last forever. An audience, however, may have been sitting or waiting in line for hours. Many competitions are now so large that even with a prejudging stage that trims down competitors to a select group, audiences are in for a long show. Large group skits, with each person recreating a specific character from one show, or "crossover" skits, with several characters from different shows (or even several versions of the same character), are popular with audiences, but even more so if they're kept quick and short. There are fewer chances to make mistakes in a quick and simple skit than in a long, complicated one with lots of special effects. Contestants do get a lot of credit for their acting prowess and imagination in these competitions, and a lot of flaws in the costumes themselves can be forgiven if the performance is good enough. Never forget that first impressions are the best ones—don't wear out your welcome!

LOOKING YOUR BEST

Most cosplay competitions take place late in the day or early in the evening as a main event, usually on Saturday, the convention's busiest day. If you are serious about taking a prize—although you can certainly enter just for the fun of it—then it's probably a very good idea not to wear your competition costume all day long. A lot of things can go wrong over the course of a day. You could spill something on your outfit during a meal, or get smudges or other marks on your costume from being squeezed together with other people in an overcrowded elevator. Your costume could get caught in a door and torn. So unless you're participating in a Hall competition, wear other clothes during the day, and be sure to leave enough extra time before the show to get dressed properly. You'll want to do a check early in the day to make sure you have everything that you'll need—did you remember a brush for hair touch-ups? Extra pins? The last thing you want to be before a competition is rushed. It will only add to your stress if you are at all nervous.

POSING

In almost all competitions, there will be one defining moment when your costume will be viewed in its best light, the moment on stage when you strike a pose. There are many different poses that any given character can take, but whichever one you choose, you should practice in a mirror until it's as perfect as you can make it. Ask your friends for their advice—another pair of eyes can help you make adjustments that you won't be able to see for yourself. Remember that the judges can see you on all sides, and posing can make or break an appearance on stage.

It is a good idea to choose a pose that you can literally step into instantly. You might think choosing a pose that takes several moments to set up would be more dramatic, but you need to consider the attention span of the audience and judges. If a show has a hundred cosplayers, and every one has an elaborate setup, then the whole show becomes drawn-out and tedious. A short, sharp pose makes an impression immediately without breaking the rhythm of the show and bogging down the flow, or losing the attention of the audience.

In the end, the most dramatic pose will often be a well-practiced one where the contestant walks out onto the stage and—BANG!—flawlessly steps right into the perfect pose without hesitation, "becoming" the character they are cosplaying.

> **Costume Awareness** Dangers abound for the catgirl in costume, far beyond rooms full of rocking chairs! Revolving doors, escalators, and other objects designed to move people about are particular concerns—a tail can easily get caught in any one of these. Go through a regular door instead of a revolving one, use the stairs or elevator instead of an escalator, although even elevators pose a danger—always make sure that your tail is clear of the closing doors. What could be more embarrassing than an elevator taking your tail (and possibly your skirt or other undergarments) up to the next floor without you? Be aware of other people, too. On a moving escalator, whoever is standing right behind you may get a flogging from your tail! Be aware of all of the space your costume takes up, and how it might interact with others.

PHOTOS

As you travel through a convention venue in costume, fans and attendees will undoubtedly ask to be allowed to take photos of you. It is more or less expected that you will say yes, as this is the custom at conventions. Fans love to take photos of cosplayers both on and off the stage, and many of these photos will later show up on cosplay or convention websites or even in print magazines. A professional photographer for publication should identify him- or herself before taking your picture, and ask you to sign some sort of release form for publication, but don't be surprised if you see pictures of yourself online posted by amateur photographers. Remember that as a cosplayer, you're considered to be part of the show at a convention.

In posing for photos, you want to remember to "hold" your pose to give photographers time to get their cameras and eyes focused on you. The best rule of thumb is to strike and hold your pose for two to three seconds. Count the time off in your head, using the usual trick of "one Mississippi—two Mississippi—three Mississippi," or some other key phrase. If you're posing with a group, you should all agree upon a time limit for holding a pose, so you'll all be in synch. Even so, be aware that hallways and other public areas can be very crowded or narrow places, and you can bring a whole hallway of people to a complete halt while photographers rush to take your picture. If getting a pose ready looks like it might take longer than literally a few seconds, stepping off to the side somewhere for a photo will be much appreciated by other convention attendees. Be courteous and ready to move on quickly once you've posed, and let the traffic flow return to normal.

On stage, the audience will be further away and in a darker lighting than in the hallways. Hold your pose for a couple of extra beats to give extra time for photographers, who won't be able to see as well or who may be shooting over the heads of the crowd. As a journalist covering cosplay competitions for well-known print magazines, I cannot tell you how many times that, after taking literally hundreds of photos at the cosplay competition, I would end up with only a couple of usable images because costumers struck their pose, held it for literally a fraction of a second, and then turned and walked off stage. Please, hold your pose!

MODESTY

Modesty can be an important issue for a costumed catgirl. It may seem a bit old-fashioned to consider modesty, but an unintentional reveal can cost you points in competition. The essence of cosplay is in your complete control over every detail of your costume and its presentation—you want to avoid anything that looks like a mistake. Even if you aren't particularly embarrassed by a flashing incident, someone else might be. Keep your audience in mind!

A stage or platform is typically placed high up, and could give an audience a view of parts of your costume you might not expect! Stepping straight to the very front of the stage might let everyone see a bit more of your costume than you want. Stay a few feet back from the edge of the stage. This should still give everyone a great view of your costume without allowing them to see up your skirt. Conventions are often held in large and lavish hotels, with steep escalators and glass elevators. Have you ever considered what the people on the ground floor might see if they happen to look up at the fancy elevator climbing the wall and you happen to be leaning against the glass wall? Likewise, you might just step onto an escalator and be casually chatting to a friend while everyone below can see exactly how your tail is attached under your skirt.

Of course, not every catgirl costume has a skirt, but if yours does, putting careful thought into your selection of undergarments will avoid most embarrassing situations. Think about wearing gym shorts, bicycle shorts, or some other type of panty-covering. Also, know every angle of the pose you are going to take and what movements it will take to get into that pose. If your pose is sitting or kneeling, you will want to practice getting there without revealing anything.

The most important thing, once again, is to be prepared. Know what you are going to do and how you're going to go about it. Not only can this keep you from giving attendees an eyeful, but it will also keep you from tripping over your own tail as you step into the spotlight.

Source Material For competitions, you'll want to make sure you have some source material on hand in case the judges ask for it. This should be a printed picture of the character wearing the costume you are recreating—a DVD insert, advertisement, manga, or other piece of official artwork (that is, assuming that you are cosplaying as an established character). Given the sheer number of titles available worldwide, it is almost impossible to expect every judge to be familiar with every character in every game, anime, or manga (not to mention the many variant versions of characters). The judge will use this image to gauge how well you have recreated the character. If you can find art showing different angles on the character—the front and back at least—so much the better. Judges might only look at one image, but it never hurts to be prepared. After all, you probably put just as much work into the back of your costume as you did the front!

RESOURCES AND GENERAL INFORMATION

All the following resources are their own entities. Neither Stone Bridge Press nor the companies listed can be held accountable for anyone else's content, opinions, or policies. The resources listed below are for reference only and are not the only possible sources for the information they contain. Inclusion or exclusion does not indicate any endorsement or lack of endorsement by Stone Bridge Press or the author of this book.

ARTWORK RESOURCES

If you're already an anime or manga fan, odds are good that you have your own best resources already, in your library of favorite manga or DVDs. The "extras" section on many anime DVDs these days features production drawings, storyboards, and character design sheets. Character design sheets are the most invaluable resource to a cosplayer, since they show a character in costume from every angle and detail.

For games, though, or more detailed color drawings of manga characters, you may want to look for reference books. Individual games, anime shows, or artist's artwork collections are worth looking into, especially if you and your friends are planning a group cosplay—everyone can make copies of the character artwork they need from a single book.

Japanese art books can be obtained through many mail order and online retailers, and are a must for any serious cosplayer. Some major cities have Japanese bookstores like Kinokuniya or Asahi Bookstore, but for the rest of the country, online retailers are the best choice. Check your local area for retailers specializing in anime, or comic book stores, since those that carry manga often also carry art books.

Anime News and Search Sites

Anime-specific resource sites can be a great help in tracking down individual anime studio websites or company sites. Many shopping sites also carry a wealth of information along with merchandise for sale, as well as news, convention listings, and forums.

Anime News Network
www.animenewsnetwork.com

Anime on DVD
www.animeondvd.com

Anime Web Turnpike
www.anipike.com

Anime News and Mail Order Sites

Many anime news sites these days also include shopping, and likewise many anime shopping sites also include news and other resources, such as convention listings, forums, reviews, even creator interviews!

Akadot
www.akadot.com

Anime Nation
www.animenation.com

The Right Stuf
www.rightstuf.com

Mail Order Sites

While you can get manga from almost any major North American bookstore these days, and order it online from major sites like Amazon, dedicated anime and manga specialty sites will often be the best places to go for hard-to-find art books or out-of-print rarities. Many specialty retailers are small operations and you can often get more personalized service than you will at a big, impersonal discount site—don't hesitate to ask for help to find what you're looking for.

This is only a starter list to anime and manga retailers. A quick online search will turn up many, many more, and don't forget to check your local area for comic book stores, or toy or game stores that carry anime or related merchandise.

Anime Castle
www.animecastle.com

Anime Gamers
www.animegamersusa.com

Anime Stop!
www.anistop.com

Books Kinokuniya
www.kinokuniya.com

Bud Plant
www.budplant.com

ChibiTokyo
www.chibitokyo.com

Joy's Japanimation
www.joysjapanimation.com

Robert's Anime Corner Store
www.animecornerstore.com

Sakura Media
www.sakuramedia.com

Wizzywig
www.wizzywig.com

U.S. Anime and Manga Translation Companies

Licensor websites are another place you can sometimes check for artwork and profiles of popular characters, including (in some cases) character sheets or even sometimes drawings of the props such as backpacks, purses, and other items. Make sure also to check for links sections on these pages—often they will lead you to some good resource pages, including Japanese studio pages.

ADV Films
www.advfilms.com

AN Entertainment
www.an-entertainment.com

AnimEigo
www.animeigo.com

Anime Works
www.animeworks.com

Bandai Entertainment
www.bandai-ent.com

Central Park Media
www.centralparkmedia.com

CMX Manga
www.dccomics.com/cmx

CPM Press
www.centralparkmedia.com/cpmpress

Dark Horse Comics
www.darkhorse.com

Del Rey
www.randomhouse.com/delrey/manga

Digital Manga Publishing
www.dmpbooks.com

DrMaster
www.drmasterbooks.com

FUNimation
www.funimation.com

Geneon
www.geneon.com

Manga Entertainment
www.manga.com

The Right Stuf International
www.rightstuf.com

TOKYOPOP
www.tokyopop.com

VIZ
www.viz.com

COSPLAY SITES AND FORUMS

Online cosplay forums, photo sites, and resource websites can be excellent sources of information as well as a way to get in touch with other cosplayers. It's great to be able to chat with other people who are as excited about cosplay as you are, and you can often ask questions and get help from more experienced cosplayers on problems you're having with your costume. Remember, though, to be polite on the forums—you'll get better responses if you're grateful and respectful of those who offer to help you!

A Fan's View
www.afansview.com

American Cosplay Paradise
www.acparadise.com

Cosplay.com
www.cosplay.com

Cosplay Lab
www.cosplaylab.com

Cosplay Photos (Obsessed With Anime)
www.cosplayphotos.com

Cosplay UK
www.cosplay.co.uk

CONVENTION SITES AND FORUMS

Nearly every anime convention these days has its own webpage, and many have a dedicated cosplay section. Make sure to check the Internet for any convention you plan to attend, and you'll probably find cosplay rules, maybe even discussion forums.

This is only a VERY small list of conventions—there are so many more, and new ones popping up every year! Be sure to check your area for events that might be happening, and check out anime resource sites for listings of new conventions!

Ai-Kon
www.ai-kon.org

A-Kon
www.a-kon.com

Ani-Magic
www.ani-magic.net

Animazment
www.animazement.org

Anime Boston
www.animeboston.com

Anime Central
www.acen.org

Anime Evolution
www.animeevolution.com

Anime Expo
www.anime-expo.org

Anime Festival Orlando
www.animefestivalorlando.com

Anime Iowa
www.animeiowa.com

Anime Mid-Atlantic
www.animemidatlantic.com

AnimeNEXT
www.animenext.org

Anime North
www.animenorth.com

Anime Weekend Atlanta
www.awa-con.com

Comic-Con International (San Diego)
www.comic-con.org

FanimeCon
www.fanime.com

Katsucon
www.katsucon.org

MechaCon
www.mechacon.com

Nan Desu Kan
www.ndkdenver.org

Ohayocon
www.ohayocon.com

Otakon
www.otakon.com

Sugoi Con
www.sugoicon.org

Wizard World (various locations)
www.wizarduniverse.com/conventions/index.cfm

GENERAL CATGIRL STUDIES

The Catgirl Research Foundation
www.catgirls.org.uk